Beer, Bread & Biscuits

Chuck the Poet

Beer, Bread & Biscuits

First published in 2017 in the UK

3P Publishing
C E C, London Road
Corby
NN17 5EU

A catalogue number for this book is available from the British Library

ISBN 978-1-911559-40-5

"You're a vegetarian? ...

You don't look like a vegetarian!"

"Beer, Bread & Biscuits."

A selection of poems by

Chuck the Poet

To one and all.
I thank you. Cheers, it's appreciated.

CONTENTS

A Short Summer

I wear my shorts in summer
Coz the legs ain't long
To don shorts in winter time
I know this would be wrong
Chilblains on my knobbly knees
I'd catch a cold and sneeze
Jack Frost would nip my ankles
My balls would feel a breeze.

Mr Beau

Mr Beau flaps his ears with glee
Hoping to disturb an irritating flea
He's standing tall, looking around
His trunk is falling to the ground

Mr Beau's big ears that flap and beat
To cool him in the mid-day heat
Eye's stare at trees with movement in
Now there's something worrying him

Mr Beau dressed in a dusty grey
From foot to foot he starts to sway
Fears arrive as a nasty smell
Across savanna, all's not well

Mr Beau, his majesty, better known as Jum
Holds his ground, he will not run
A gun is fired, the beast is stunned
A cry, a shout, but worse to come

Mr Beau's not dead, lies in the dirt
Three men approach wanting to hurt
Kalashnikov poised, aim to hit
But from above a rifle whip

Mr Beau looks up, the assailants too
A hovering chopper, ranger and his crew
They're here to save, help out old Jum
Protect the wildlife that's why they've come

To stop the muggers, such evil men
A passion of greed controlling them
To kill for tusks, and sent to ground
One gang stopped more must be found

Mr Jum Beau's saved, free and he's still here
But the threat on elephants won't disappear
Don't buy ivory, trade in or consume
Or the death of the elephant will be very soon.

Lick

I want to lick
To lick your lobe
To lick it hard
And lick it long
I must not stop

(pause)

Or do it wrong

I want to delve
Go round the bend
My tongue is moist
Suck till the end

To rummage about
In your lug 'ole
To go down deep
And deeper still
Lap at your flaps
'ere's sexual thrill

But a part sticks
To tongue it's stuck
It enters my mouth
Urgh yuck

A lobe to lick
With dampish suck
An ear to pick
Don't like my luck
For this conclusion
I'll give to you

Earwax !

Is not good

To chew...

The Woodlouse

A terrestrial isopod crustacean

There's a Woodlouse in the bathroom
It crawled along the wall
I flicked it with my finger
It rolled into a ball

They All Popped Their Clogs

In the front room first the cat died
Then the budgie popped his clogs
Followed by Iggy
The iguana
And Bill
One of the dogs

But it weren't till Uncle Ted passed by
Whilst consumed with guilt and gloom
We asked ourselves
The question
"Why's it called the living room?"

2CV

I've got a Citroën 2CV
No hitchers wanna ride with me
My mates think I'm the laughing stock
But the micky takings gonna stop
See my car's great
Wheels? It's got four
A cracked sunroof
And creaky door
Battered wing
Broken front light
Which means I can't go out at night
Me? I don't care
At least it goes
My love for it just grows and grows
Low petrol intake
That's a fact
Greenpeace would be pleased with that
Super amazing, mechanical sound
Though the exhaust scrapes the ground
It's white and green and burgundy too
A sticky clutch, scent of mildew
Patched in stereo, ripped back seat
But I've gotta say it's really neat
I love my car and my car is me
I love that Citroën 2CV

On Warm Eddies

Watch me flick my boggy
On warm eddies it will fly
If my sister hadn't worn glasses
It would have hit her in the eye

Corby Taxis

Clear way madness
Hand break scream
Black Hackney carriages
Corby's taxi team

Honking on corners
Causing a din
Corby taxi drivers
Getting fares in

Late night travel trip
Picking up at pubs
Drop off up the Shire
Back to catch the clubs

Crisp twenty early evening
All they do is moan
Sometimes a Corby taxi ride
Makes you wish you'd stayed at home

Dashing round town centre
Like proverbial busy bees
Can't flag one when you want one
When you don't they're seen in threes

Corby taxi drivers like
To race down the bypass
Under take on the slipway
Just miss the verge of grass

Always nice to see the rank
Is lined up in a queue
Of Corby taxis ready to roll
For that's is what they do

One or two a menace
On the open road
Cutting up on corners
Don't know the Highway Code

Of course Corby taxi drivers
Will always get you there
Or else you're dumped in Gretton
For not having the fare

But don't forget the black cabs
That ferry you at night
To get to where you're going
Corby taxis deliver just right

On The Edge of the Beach and the Break (Water)

You said
"The sand that is ours will be lost to the ocean"
You said that to me
As we stare at the sea
At the edge of the world
Or was it Exmouth?
As a reply
To be clever
A retort
I thought
And said "she sells sea shells on the sea shore" and laughed
As if it had never be heard before
But I was 34
And after a beer
In Exmoor
At the Blue Bore
You swore
Under your breath
Unfunny!
I grab for your hand
And fail to land
My fingers in yours
Desperately I try again
And as your hand holds mine
It feels like you
Wish I was someone else
We drove home
In silence
Conversation taken
By the sea
No kiss. Goodbye
An Ex-mouth
Wanting

Don Boston

Don, Don, Don Boston
Cuts my hair
Where?
There!
In the chair
For its long
Feeling greasy
Don't split hairs
Wash it there!
Where?
In the sink
So it's clean
Don't use Vosene

Don, Don, Don Boston
Cut my hair
Now!
How?
Make it Wow!
Offer style
With scissors and comb

Coz it's grown
Cut it here
Cut it there
Use some gel
Brylcream too
And if you need to
Spray with glue!

Don, Don, Don Boston
Cuts my hair
Yeah?
Yeah!!
He takes care
In his shop
Gorgeous looks
Now I'm cool
A cut that's new
With nice shampoo
Great finish
Now I'm gone
Thanks to Don Boston

The Conker Conquer

...a poem for Southwick, Northants.

To conquer in the contest
My conker conks to win
Controlled conditioned strike
Tight strings
Big knot
Begin

Condone the contestant's Chestnut
Victor breaks in half his foe
Confronted in the conflict
Of the greatest conker show

A Common Sense Poem

...for Bedtime

Do not wear your glasses
When tucked safely in your bed
As you may just roll over
And they'd be crushed by your head

Handle...get a life
Get a handle

I think
What it needs
Is a handle

It doesn't matter where
But somewhere
Anywhere
A fix
A handle

Even if you know
You won't be strolling off
Picking up
Popping out for walks
Or carrying it
Slap on
A handle

Make it complete
Unabridged
Whole
Totally finished
Add
A handle

Many permanent fixtures and fittings
Have handles

Perfectly permanently fitted
And fixed
Forever
Stood still
Never to move
Stuck
Still stood still
Later in time
Still set still
Many years on
And there's nothing wrong
Coz it's got a handle

Most objects
Have a handle

Even stairs
Commonly known as
Bannisters
But it's a handle to me

Me
Yes!
Me, I have handles
Love handles

Unfortunately
No one loves me
But it useful to know
If you wanna go
You can pick me up

I've got accommodating handles

If handles are built in
Build them up
Handles have power
Power to the handles

And handling handles
Is hot and sexy
Fingers fingering
The handle
Handling
Gripping
Grappling
At and round
A handle

A better invention that the wheel?
I feel
Yes, and international renowned
Plus not a bad composer
I toast a
Handle

Skinny Dipping

In freezing conditions
It’s ever so bold
To go skinny dipping
In a river that’s cold
You could catch a sneeze
Or a terrible cough
Your extremities freeze
And may even fall off

M. I. L. F.

Ever since you dumped me baby
I said I'd get you back
By logging on that website
Chat up ya Mum and that
I'll Instagram and poke her
Snapchat her on my space
I know how much you'll hate it
When I come across her Face

Book

Profile

Blinking Light

Blinkin' light
Blinkin' outside my window
Blinkin' on
Blinkin' off
Blinkin' on
Blinkin' off
Blinkin' on
Blinkin' off
Blinkin' all night
Blinkin' light
Blinkin' Council might
Blinkin' fix it. Too
Blinkin' tight
Blinkin' nightmare
Blinkin' nuisance
Blinkin' light

The Late Late Drinking Show

It was one of those nights
Of too many beers
A couple of shots
I was up to my ears
With the bottles and pints
But I had to get home
So I called up a cab
On my mobile phone
That's easier said
That actually done
My head is spinning
It really ain't fun
But the taxi ride's short
The driver's paid quick
I'm needing to move
I'm feeling well sick
Getting into the house
That takes me an age
Then stumble up stairs
And slip on a page
Of the latest lads mag
I'd read in the loo
I really can't focus
Only one thing to do
So I'm down on my knees
I can't close my eyes
The floors on the ceiling
It all starts to rise

In my guts
I lunge
I wretch
And I heave
It’s mostly all liquid
With carrots,
Believe me
It's never pleasant
That smell that arrives
When it all hits the pan
And feels like your lives
Over and done with
I'm needing my bed
But a bloke with a hammer
Is inside my head
I'm feeling like shit
As my eyes start to close
With that taste in my mouth
And the stench on my clothes
I'm only half dressed
Just wearing one shoe
Its dark and I'm spinning
And I still wanna spew
Till I've fallen asleep
I'm out of it then
To wake in the morning
Never again.

Shoes

Ode to Northamptonshire.
The Capital of Cobblers

Northamptonshire's the centre
Of the industry of shoes
Where many are made
In styles and shapes
And colours just
For you to choose
See, shoes are really useful
Designed and made with care
And all the folk of
Northamptonshire
Seem to have a pair

This is called...

A holiday destination in a far off, verdant and lush South East Asian country. The expectation of hot and sticky weather but with the gentle mountain winds to chill the soul, relax the mind and rebuild the body. An escape. Buddhist monks will walk the dusty streets, orange sashes sway and the scent of jasmine rides on the air, but until we land the view of the mountains and the thick milk chocolate river below is all we can see from the window of the plane as the landing gear is released. Below the jungle almost grows up to meet us. As we fly through the air we are reminded of the primates, Honey Bears, small eared Asian Elephants as well pythons and vipers that roam the vegetation, and hide in temple gardens and monastery's that we too will have time to discover once the plane lands and we reach our destination. I stare out of the window. It's difficult to turn my gaze away from the wonderland that fills my eyes.

So with this in mind I wrote the following poem.

WOW!
LAOS

If you pronounced it lay-oss, try it again.